# WHAT DO YOU KNOW ABOUT

# FEELING VIOLENT

## PETE SANDERS

## COPPER BEECH BOOKS

### BROOKFIELD, CONNECTICUT

Designed and produced by
Aladdin Books Ltd
28 Percy Street
London W1P 0LD

First published
in the United States in 1997 by
Copper Beech Books,
an imprint of
The Millbrook Press
2 Old New Milford Road
Brookfield, Connecticut 06804

Printed in Belgium

The publishers wish to thank all
the children and adults who posed
for the photographs in this book.

Design          David West
                Children's
                Book Design
Designers       Flick Killerby
                Keith Newell
Editor          Jen Green
Picture research Emma Krikler
Illustrator     Mike Lacy

Library of Congress
Cataloging-in-Publication Data
Sanders, Pete.
Feeling violent / Pete Sanders and Steve
Myers; illustrated by Mike Lacey.
p. cm. -- (What do you know about)
Includes index.
ISBN 0-7613-0700-1 (lib. bdg.)
1. Violence--United States--Juvenile
literature.  2. Violent crimes--United
States--Juvenile literature. I. Myers, Steve.
II. Lacey, Mike. III. Title. IV. Series:
Sanders, Pete.  What do you know about.
HN90.V5S26 1997          97-10354
303.6--dc21              CIP

5 4 3 2 1

# CONTENTS

## HOW TO USE THIS BOOK

*The books in this series are intended to help young people to understand more about issues that may affect their lives. Each book can be read by a child alone, or together with a parent, teacher, or helper, so that there is an opportunity to talk through ideas as they come up. The questions that appear on the storyline pages throughout the book are intended to invite further discussion.*

*At the end of the book there is a section called "What Can We Do?" This section provides practical ideas that will be useful for both young people and adults, as well as a list of names and addresses for further information and support.*

# INTRODUCTION

WE ARE ALL AFFECTED BY VIOLENCE IN OUR LIVES. WE MAY HAVE SEEN VIOLENCE HAPPEN. WE MAY EVEN HAVE EXPERIENCED IT OURSELVES.

**You have probably felt violent yourself at some time or other. It is hard to deal with your feelings when this happens.**
This book will help you find out more about the causes and effects of violence. Each chapter introduces a different aspect of the subject, illustrated by an episode in a continuing story. The characters in the story feel and act in ways you may find familiar. After each episode we stop and look at some of the issues raised, and broaden the discussion. Ways of dealing with violent feelings are suggested. By the end you will understand more about why violence happens, and what can be done about it.

# WHAT IS VIOLENCE ?

WATCHING THE NEWS ON TV, OR READING A NEWSPAPER RECENTLY, YOU HAVE PROBABLY SEEN REPORTS OF VIOLENCE.

## Violence means any act of force that harms people or property.

If you fight, or threaten to hit someone, you are behaving violently. Bullies at school often use violence to try to get others to act in the way they want, or to hand over money or property. People who behave like this have planned to be violent. Their actions do not happen on the spur of the moment, but are thought about beforehand.

## Violence can also flare up suddenly.

If you have ever lost your temper yourself, you know that this can happen very quickly. Some people have a very bad temper, which they find impossible to control. When people like that become angry, they can be frightening, and may hurt others.

Sometimes bullies get their way simply by threatening to use violence.

I'VE DONE MINE ABOUT THE FACTORY FIRE. FIVE PEOPLE WERE KILLED.

I CHOSE THAT CASE ABOUT THE TWO KIDS WHO BEAT UP AN OLD LADY. ONE OF THEM WAS ONLY NINE.

▽ The whole class knew about Beverley's news story. One of the boys lived in the neighborhood.

WHY DO YOU THINK THOSE CHILDREN WOULD DO SOMETHING LIKE THIS?

MY DAD SAYS IT'S THE PARENTS' FAULT, AND THEY SHOULD BE LOCKED AWAY TOO.

△ Beverley and her friend Carol were discussing their homework. They had to write about a news story.

MY MOM'S FRIEND TOLD HER THOSE KIDS HAD BEEN UP TO NO GOOD FOR YEARS, BUT NOBODY DID ANYTHING ABOUT IT.

GIRL, 10, BOY, 9 QUESTIONED ABOUT BRUTAL BEATING

◁ At recess, Beverley and Carol couldn't stop thinking about the case.

▽ Beverley had seen Cliff with new toys that she knew he could not afford.

I'D TELL ON HIM IF I COULD PROVE IT.

CLIFF'S ALWAYS SKIPPING SCHOOL, AND HANGING AROUND WITH HIS BROTHER'S GANG. DO YOU THINK HE MIGHT END UP LIKE THOSE OTHER TWO?

IT WOULDN'T SURPRISE ME. I KNOW FOR A FACT HE DAMAGES PROPERTY.

I DON'T THINK WE SHOULD SAY ANYTHING. I'M SCARED OF HIM. HE'S GOT AN AWFUL TEMPER.

The girls watched Cliff and his friend bullying another boy. Cliff was always in trouble for fighting.

**Do you think Beverley and Carol should tell on Cliff?**

**Cliff is an example of someone who uses violence to get his own way.**
You may know someone like him with a reputation for having a fierce temper. This reputation makes others afraid to do anything about his bullying.

**Most acts of violence are also crimes.**
A crime is any action that is forbidden by law. Laws are made by governments to protect people and property. The job of the police is to ensure laws are obeyed, and to catch people who break them.

**There are many kinds of crime.**
Crimes range from murder and theft to dropping litter and causing a nuisance by being noisy. Hitting someone is a crime called "assault." It is worrying that more and more criminals, including some young people, now use violence when they commit crimes.

**Vandalism is a kind of violence.**
It is any action that deliberately damages property. Some acts of vandalism are done to try to upset a particular person. Often, though, people damage something if they are jealous because they don't own it themselves. Sometimes vandals say they are just fooling around. If accused of damaging property, Cliff might try to excuse himself in this way.

# WHY DO PEOPLE USE VIOLENCE?

THERE ARE MANY DIFFERENT REASONS WHY PEOPLE ACT VIOLENTLY.

**Some young people use violence when they want to look big or impress others.**

It may be that they are joining in to be part of a gang, or that they are copying someone they look up to. Others are violent because they hold a grudge, or think they can scare people into doing what they want.

Some parents behave violently toward children, even very young babies, when they are feeling impatient or under great stress. When this happens, violence becomes the world the child knows. Children who have been treated violently from a very early age may believe that violence is perfectly natural. They may go on to use violence themselves, because they do not know how else to express their feelings, and have never learned to communicate in other ways.

Some adults use their greater size and strength to force children to do what they want them to.

The next day....

THAT SHOULD TEACH THEM TO BUY AN EXPENSIVE CAR.

HEY, JEFF'S BROUGHT CLIFF - HE'LL MAKE A GREAT LOOKOUT.

Cliff's brother, Jeff, was the leader of a gang. The gang was always getting into trouble, but Cliff liked it when he was allowed to go along with Jeff.

I'M NOT SURE I WANT TO DO THIS.

OK, COUNT ME IN.

1

▷ The gang explained the plan to Cliff.

2

◁ Cliff kept watch as the gang stole Jack's bike.

▽ Jeff was pleased with Cliff.

I HOPE THEY WON'T BE LONG.

3

HEY, LEAVE ME ALONE. YOU'RE NOT TAKING MY BIKE.

SAYS WHO?

4

NEXT TIME I'LL USE THE KNIFE.

5

YOU'VE DONE WELL TODAY CLIFF. YOU'LL SOON BE A REAL MEMBER OF THE GANG.

THEN I'LL HAVE A KNIFE TOO.

6

▷ Jack was punched and left on the pavement.

**Why do you think Cliff went along with the gang?**

8

**Some people enjoy the feeling of trying to get away with something they should not be doing.**
Like Cliff, it may be that they start off by doing little things they know are wrong. If they do not get caught, they may be tempted to try even more daring things.

**Cliff looks up to his brother, Jeff, and often copies him.**
When you admire someone very much, you want them to like you too. It can be difficult to recognize that some of their actions are wrong. You may find yourself going along with them to win their approval or friendship.

**People who intend to be violent often choose an "easy target" as their victim, so that they are more likely to get away with their actions.**
Jeff and his gang knew that Jack would be alone. Jack was greatly outnumbered, and Jeff threatened him with a knife.

**Some people get into trouble because they are bored.**
They may try to excuse some kinds of violence, such as vandalism, by saying that there is nothing else for them to do. This is particularly a problem among young people, and many adults want more money to be spent on providing activities and youth clubs that will help prevent them from becoming bored.

# GANGS

GANGS GO AROUND TOGETHER BECAUSE IT CAN BE FUN TO BE PART OF A GROUP. SOMETIMES, THOUGH, GANG MEMBERS WILL DARE EACH OTHER, AND THIS CAN LEAD TO TROUBLE.

**Some gangs attract people who want to appear tough.**
Gang members may try to prove how tough they are by challenging other gangs. You may have heard of "gang warfare," when rival gangs fight each other. This happens when gang members believe a fight will prove their gang is better in some way.

**Some gangs have very strict rules.**
For example, they may decide that nobody from another gang is allowed to walk down a certain street, or play in a particular area. If others break their "rules," there may be a fight. Often people who go around in gangs find it hard to refuse to join in with what the rest are doing. The pressure to go along with what is happening can be very strong. Going against the crowd often takes great courage.

When you are part of a gang, it can be easy to forget that you have a right to your own opinion.

**JEFF AND THAT GROUP BEAT ME UP AND STOLE MY BIKE. HE HAD A KNIFE.**

**HE LIKES TO THINK HE'S TOUGH. WE'LL SEE ABOUT THAT. YOU LEAVE THIS TO ME.**

◁ Jack didn't go to the police. He had a better idea. He went to find Roland, his sister's boyfriend.

▽ Roland jumped on Cliff outside the shop.

**I HEAR YOUR BROTHER LIKES PICKING ON LITTLE KIDS. YOU TELL HIM FROM ME – THERE'S GOING TO BE TROUBLE.**

The next day...

**HOW MUCH ARE THE ONES AT THE TOP THERE, PLEASE?**

△ While the shopkeeper's back was turned, Cliff grabbed some chocolate.

That evening...

**DON'T WORRY ABOUT ROLAND. HE LIKES TO THINK HE'S TOUGH, BUT IT'S ALL JUST SHOW.**

▷ When Jeff told his girlfriend Sue about Roland's threat, she laughed.

◁ The next day, Jeff told Cliff that the gang was going to straighten out Roland.

**THIS IS AS FAR AS YOU GO. YOU'RE TOO YOUNG TO GET INVOLVED IN THIS.**

**I DON'T LIKE THIS AT ALL. THEY SAY ROLAND EVEN SCRATCHES CARS. BE CAREFUL.**

As the gangs fought, several people were hurt as they tried to get out of the way.

**Should Jack have gone to the police?**

11

### Revenge can often lead to violence.

Sometimes people are violent because they want to get back at others. Jack and Roland's desire for revenge led to a gang fight. Instead of solving anything, fighting made the situation worse. The boys are now even less likely to see each other's point of view.

### When situations get out of control, it can be difficult to remember that other people are individuals, with feelings just as important as your own.

You can begin to see others as your "enemy," without thinking about their reasons for disagreeing with you. This can be particularly true if you are part of a gang.

### It is not a good idea to take the law into your own hands.

You can't always predict what will happen, and could find yourself in a lot of trouble. If Jack had talked to an adult he trusted, or had gone to the police, the outcome would have been very different.

### Jeff and Roland have not thought about the consequences of their actions.

During the fight, other people who happened to be in the area were hurt. Often people who are violent do not think about how their victims and others may be affected.

# LIVING WITH VIOLENCE

IN SOME FAMILIES THERE ARE ADULTS WHO ARE VIOLENT WITH EACH OTHER, AND WITH THEIR CHILDREN.

**These people are often able to get away with violence because the others involved are too afraid to tell anyone about it.**

The reasons for the violence are not always obvious. Although family members are the ones who suffer, the anger may be caused by something outside. People who cannot get a job, or who worry about not having enough money to get by, may become angry and hurt those closest to them. People who are very unhappy with their lives may use violence to take out their feelings on others. The person who is being violent needs help. Problems often arise because people refuse to admit they need help, or do not know how to get it.

Some people become violent when they have been drinking alcohol.

A week later...

1. YOU SHOULDN'T HAVE GOT CAUGHT. I WON'T HAVE THE POLICE AROUND HERE. THEY ALWAYS TAKE SIDES AGAINST PEOPLE LIKE US.

IT WASN'T MY FAULT. YOU'RE ALWAYS PICKING ON ME.

△ The gang leaders had been recognized. Jeff and Roland were both cautioned by the police.

▷ Roland hated his parents arguing. He and his friend Mark went to find their friend Steven.

▽ Roland's father did not like the police being involved. He had been drinking and became angry.

2. YOU'RE BOTH AS BAD AS EACH OTHER. ROLAND'S LUCKY TO GET OFF WITH A WARNING.

3. I'VE HAD ENOUGH OF THIS. I'M GOING OUT.

DON'T GO GETTING INTO MORE TROUBLE. A WARNING IS SERIOUS YOU KNOW.

4. HEY, YOU'RE JUST IN TIME. COME WITH ME. I'VE GOT A GREAT PLAN.

▷ Steven explained his plan to the others.

5. WHY NOT? IT'S ONE WAY OF LEARNING TO DRIVE.

COUNT ME OUT. I THINK YOU'RE CRAZY.

THERE'S NO ONE COMING. HURRY UP.

I HOPE YOU KNOW HOW TO START ONE OF THESE.

◁ Despite what everyone thought, this was the first time Roland had stolen a car himself.

▷ They sped off through the streets. Roland was excited. He had been drinking and found it hard to keep the car under control.

◁ Roland heard a siren, and increased his speed. He suddenly felt very angry. He'd show the police.

OH NO!

▷ Roland twisted the wheel sharply. The car mounted the pavement. He didn't see the woman until it was too late.

## Alcohol alters the way we think and feel.

Many people enjoy a drink. However, like Roland's father, some people become aggressive after they have been drinking. This can lead to violence. Too much alcohol makes you drunk. People who are drunk are not fully in control of their actions, but they may not be aware that alcohol is affecting them in this way. This is why there are strict laws about not driving after drinking alcohol. Some people, like Roland, become reckless when they drink, and may do something they wouldn't do if they were sober.

## Alcohol can become a habit – called "addiction."

Some people come to rely on alcohol and believe they cannot do without it. At its worst this kind of addiction can rule their lives.

## If someone in a family is addicted to alcohol, both family and friends will be affected too.

Roland went out because his father had been drinking and had become violent. It is unfortunate that people who are trying to escape violent situations at home may sometimes find themselves getting into other kinds of trouble.

# IS THERE MORE CRIME & VIOLENCE NOW·THAN THERE USED TO BE?

THERE SEEM TO BE MORE AND MORE REPORTS OF CRIME AND VIOLENCE THESE DAYS, PARTICULARLY AMONG YOUNG PEOPLE.

**No one knows why this is. It may be simply that more violence and crime are reported, and because nearly everyone has a television or radio, we hear more about it now than we used to.**

Television itself has also been blamed for the increase in crime and violence. It has been suggested that too many violent programs appear, and that advertisements show a glamorous world which many people want, but cannot afford. Some people think it is the fault of adults for being less strict than they used to be, and allowing children to get away with too much. They believe adults need to help children understand that violence and crime are not acceptable.

Some adults believe that the world was a safer place in the old days. Not everyone agrees with this idea.

YOU KNOW YOU'RE IN A LOT OF TROUBLE, DON'T YOU? YOU MIGHT HAVE KILLED THAT WOMAN.

I NEVER MEANT TO HURT ANYONE. SHE CAME OUT OF NOWHERE.

Roland's lawyer explained the situation to him.

◁ After the crash, Steven had run away before the police arrived. Roland was arrested. The woman had been badly injured.

THE POLICE ARE ALWAYS ARRESTING PEOPLE FOR NOTHING.

YOU'VE COMMITTED A SERIOUS CRIME.

IT WASN'T MY IDEA IN THE FIRST PLACE. I ALWAYS GET BLAMED FOR EVERYTHING. IT WAS THE SAME WHEN I WAS AT SCHOOL.

YOU COULD GO TO PRISON FOR WHAT YOU'VE DONE. THE COURT MIGHT GO EASIER ON YOU IF YOU TOLD US WHO WAS WITH YOU.

I DON'T TELL ON MY FRIENDS.

OKAY, INSPECTOR. MY CLIENT SAYS HE WAS IN THE CAR WITH JEFF STANWAY.

YOU CERTAINLY SEEM TO HAVE GOT A REPUTATION FOR CAUSING TROUBLE.

HEY, I WAS NO ANGEL. BUT IF ANYTHING WENT WRONG I WAS THE FIRST ONE THEY CAME TO. IT'S THE SAME WITH THE POLICE.

△ But Roland suddenly had an idea how he could get back at Jeff.

### Roland has a reputation for always being in trouble.

Some people think it is important to appear tough all the time. They want to impress others or be accepted by them. This can lead to them being blamed for something they did not do. As Roland has found out, once people have formed an opinion about you, it can be very difficult to make them see what you are really like.

### People sometimes use violence to hide how they are really feeling.

They may be afraid of someone finding out they are not good at something. We already know that Roland cannot read properly. People like him may become angry and refuse to do something, hoping that others will notice only their anger.

They may throw a temper tantrum to get out of having to do something they cannot do well.

### Some adults believe that being exposed to violence can make people act violently.

There is more violence on television, in films, and in newspapers than there used to be. Some people think watching violent programs makes us accept violence more easily. Others disagree. Whatever you think, it is important to remember that what you are watching is often make-believe. It may look exciting. But trying to copy what you see on screen could lead to someone being hurt for real.

# FEELING ANGRY

EVERYONE FEELS ANGRY FROM TIME TO TIME. IT IS SOMETIMES VERY DIFFICULT TO HANDLE YOUR TEMPER. THE FEELINGS YOU HAVE ARE STRONG, AND IT MAY SEEM IMPOSSIBLE NOT TO ACT ON THEM.

**There is nothing wrong with feeling angry, but it is important to learn to control your temper.**

If you are having an argument with someone, it may be frustrating if you are not given the chance to answer back, or express your own point of view. You may feel very annoyed, and perhaps be tempted to take it out on someone else.

**Anger can flare up quickly, but it often goes away just as fast.**

Leaving a situation for a few minutes can help. You will then be able to judge the situation more clearly. Even if you think you are in the right, it is sometimes best to wait before reacting. If you do something in anger, you may regret it later.

Sometimes when we are angry, we take it out on people who may not be to blame.

Two days later...

I'VE NEVER SEEN CLIFF CRY BEFORE.

IT'S UNDERSTANDABLE. WE SHOULD TALK TO HIM. HE REALLY BELIEVES JEFF DIDN'T DO IT.

◁ Beverley and Carol had heard about Jeff's arrest. He had not had an alibi for the night of the crash.

I'M GOING TO GET THAT ROLAND.

WHERE WILL THAT GET YOU? YOU'D JUST BE IN TROUBLE TOO.

THE POLICE DON'T ARREST PEOPLE FOR NOTHING. IF JEFF DIDN'T DO ANYTHING IT WILL ALL BE OKAY.

HE DIDN'T DO IT. I HATE ROLAND AND I HATE THE POLICE

◁ The two girls tried to reason with Cliff. But Cliff wouldn't listen.

▷ Cliff started to fight with Carol.

YOU'RE JUST UPSET. WHAT ABOUT THE WOMAN WHO WAS KNOCKED DOWN? SHE'S THE ONE YOU SHOULD THINK ABOUT.

I SHOULD HAVE KNOWN YOU'D TAKE THEIR SIDE. GET LOST!

YOU THINK YOU KNOW EVERYTHING.

OW!

YOU LET GO OF HER!

Beverley suddenly felt very angry, and began to hit Cliff.

**Do you think Beverley was right to hit Cliff?**

21

As Beverley, Cliff, and Carol are learning, fighting usually causes more problems than it solves.
Using physical violence will not help you to sort out a problem. In the heat of the moment it can also be easy to hurt somebody badly, without meaning to do so. It can be very difficult to stand back. But learning to do this can help prevent violence sometimes.

**Discussions are useful. However, one person shouting at another is rarely helpful.**
If you disagree with someone, it is always best to say what you think calmly, and give reasons. But you must also be prepared to really listen to what the other person is saying.

**Cliff was already feeling angry when the girls approached him.**
Recognizing when someone may be angry, and trying not to provoke them further, can help to stop some situations from becoming violent.

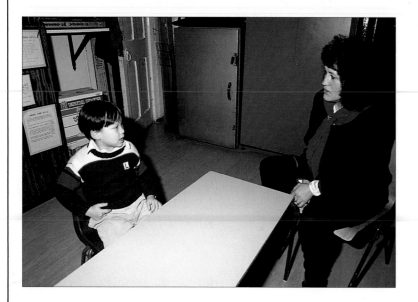

**Talking about your feelings can help to sort out problems.**
If you bottle things up and don't discuss them, you will probably feel worse. Many people find that a problem is not as bad as they thought once they start to talk about it. Another person may have ideas about how to handle a difficult situation.

# TAKING RESPONSIBILITY

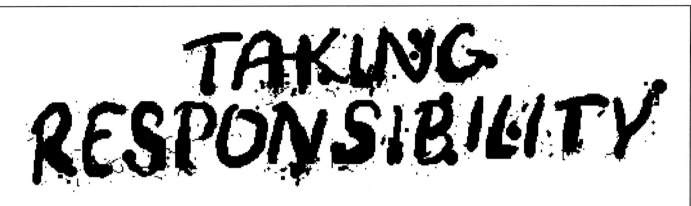

YOU MAY HAVE HEARD FRIENDS SAY THAT SOMEONE ELSE MADE THEM DO SOMETHING THEY ARE IN TROUBLE FOR. YOU MAY EVEN HAVE USED THIS EXCUSE YOURSELF, TO AVOID TAKING THE BLAME FOR SOMETHING.

**As we grow older, most of us realize that we must be responsible for what we say and do.**

We learn that blaming others for our behavior is not right. It is likely that there have been times in your life when you went along with what others were doing, even though you didn't want to. It can be difficult to refuse to do something if everyone else is joining in. Saying no to something you know is wrong is hard, especially if you are being threatened, or think you may lose a friendship. Most people are scared of being rejected. Yet if you don't say no, you may end up not respecting yourself.

Often you will gain respect by speaking your mind, and not just going along with the gang. You may even find that others feel the way you do, but were afraid to speak up.

◁ Mrs. Anderson took them inside and asked what had happened. Beverley blamed Cliff.

▽ Beverley thought a lot about what Mrs. Anderson had said about different kinds of violence.

▷ Mrs. Anderson talked to them for a while, and tried to help them see each other's point of view.

**There are very few people who could say that they have never felt violent at some time in their lives.**
As with Beverley, this does not necessarily make them violent people. It is important to find ways of handling violent feelings, so that situations don't get out of control.

**It is helpful to try to understand how other people are feeling.**
Mrs. Anderson helped Beverley, Carol, and Cliff to realize that we don't all see situations in the same way all the time. If you want people to respect you, you must remember that they want to be respected too. You must be prepared to listen to their side of the story.

**There are times when we all have to own up to being in the wrong.**
This can be very difficult. But if you continue to defend your actions, as Cliff and Beverley did at first, the situation will not improve.

**Some feelings are easy to talk about. Others are more difficult.**
It can often be hard to understand why we are feeling the way we are at a particular moment. We all have lots of different feelings, and as Beverley found out, they can sometimes take us by surprise.

# HOW CAN WE STOP VIOLENCE?

PEOPLE HAVE LOTS OF DIFFERENT IDEAS ABOUT HOW TO PREVENT VIOLENCE.

**By now, you may have ideas of your own about this.**
Some people think that violence would be reduced if there were even tougher punishments for violent crimes. This might make people think twice about being violent again. Those who are violent need to appreciate the effect their actions have on their victims. Perhaps violent people would change the way they behave if they had a better understanding of the suffering they cause. Some adults believe that young people need to be taught about the problem of violence from an early age, so that children learn not to accept violence as a natural way of behaving.

If you are feeling angry, it can sometimes be helpful to channel your energy into sports.

Some months later...

**1** WELL I GUESS ROLAND WILL BE OUT OF TROUBLE FOR A WHILE.

I'M GLAD THEY FOUND OUT THE TRUTH ABOUT JEFF.

◁ Roland had finally admitted in court that Jeff was not involved. Jeff had been released.

**2** IT'S CLIFF I FEEL SORRY FOR. HE WAS SO MUCH BETTER WHEN JEFF WASN'T AROUND.

HE'S FOUND SOME NEW FRIENDS NOW. I THINK HE'LL BE ALRIGHT.

▽ When Beverley's mom returned from shopping, Carol told her what they had been talking about.

**3** PRISON'S TOO GOOD FOR PEOPLE LIKE ROLAND. THEY'RE TOO SOFT ON THEM IN THERE.

I AGREE WITH CAROL. I THINK ROLAND SHOULD BE MADE TO HELP OUT OTHER PEOPLE, NOT JUST PUT IN PRISON.

▽ Mrs. Anderson told the class they could have a short discussion about the case.

HOW ARE YOU CLIFF? I HEAR YOU'RE USING UP YOUR ENERGY PLAYING SPORTS NOW.

▽ Now the case was in the news again, everyone at school was talking about it.

I WANT EVERYONE TO BE QUIET.

**4** I THINK IT'S GREAT. IT MUST HAVE BEEN FUN DRIVING THAT CAR.

YES, BUT THAT WOMAN STILL CAN'T WALK PROPERLY.

**5** YES MISS. I PLAY FOOTBALL TWICE A WEEK. I GO TO A CLUB.

▽ Mrs. Anderson brought the subject back to Roland.

▽ Mrs. Anderson was pleased with Beverley's response.

**The class have begun to come up with their own ideas about how violence can be stopped.**
Many schools use the local police to talk to young people about crime and violence and what can be done about them. They can also give advice about how to stay out of trouble.

**Some people think that being punished will make young people think carefully about their actions in future.**
Have you ever been smacked for doing something naughty? Some adults believe that physical punishment does no harm, and makes children less likely to get into trouble. Others disagree. They believe that young people need to be taught to understand situations for themselves. Then they will choose not to do something because they know it is wrong, not just because they are frightened of getting caught and punished.

**Not everyone agrees that punishment alone changes the way people behave.**
Beverley now understands that learning a job in prison might help Roland when he is released. Roland got into trouble partly because he was bored and unhappy. People like him need help to change the circumstances that led to their turning to crime and violence, so that they are not tempted to repeat their actions.

# WHAT CAN WE DO?

HAVING READ THIS BOOK, YOU WILL UNDERSTAND MORE ABOUT THE CAUSES AND EFFECTS OF VIOLENCE.

**By now you will probably have your own thoughts about how you can help to prevent violence.**

It is important to judge each situation carefully. Avoiding circumstances when violence might happen can often prevent a problem before it begins. You have learned a lot about different ways to handle feelings. If you are feeling violent yourself, talking about it with someone you can trust, and not acting on the spur of the moment, will help. You may want to put your energy into playing a sport, or go for a run until you have calmed down. If you are experiencing problems to do with crime or violence, and are unsure who to talk to, some of the organizations listed on these pages will be able to help.

**National Clearinghouse on Child Abuse and Neglect Information**
330 Charles Street
Washington, DC 20201
Tel: 800-394-3366

**Parents and Teachers Against Violence in Education**
P.O. Box 1033
Alamo, CA 94507-7033
Tel: 510-831-1661

**Center for Nonviolent Communication**
P.O. Box 2662
Sherman, TX 75091
Tel: 903-893-3886

VIOLENCE AFFECTS EVERYONE – NOT JUST THE PEOPLE WHO ARE BEING VIOLENT AND THEIR VICTIMS. THOSE WHO KNOW ABOUT IT, OR WHO WATCH IT HAPPEN, ARE AFFECTED TOO.

**Sometimes adults too need help with problems involving crime and violence.**

Many of the organizations listed below can help both adults and children – those who use violence and those who have been treated violently. Adults and children who have read this book together may find it helpful to share their own ideas and experiences of violence. Nobody should have to put up with violence. Together we can help to stop it.

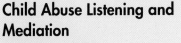

**Child Abuse Listening and Mediation**
P.O. Box 90754
Santa Barbara,
CA 93190-0754
Tel: 805-965-2376

**American Humane Association–Child Division**
63 Inverness Drive E.
Englewood,
CO 80112-5117
Tel: 800-227-4645

**National Safe Kids Campaign**
111 Michigan Ave, NW
Washington, DC 20010
Tel: 202-884-4993

**Children's Creative Response to Conflict Program**
c/o Fellowship of Reconciliation
521 N. Broadway
Box 271
Nyack, NY 10960
Tel: 914-353-1746

**Kids' Rights**
10100 Park Cedar Drive
Charlotte, NC 28210
Tel: 800-892-5437

**Children's Rights Council**
2201 I Street, NE
Suite 230
Washington, DC 20002
Tel: 800-787-KIDS

**National Council on Child Abuse and Family Violence**
1155 Connecticut Ave, NW
Suite 400
Washington, DC 20036
Tel: 800-222-2000

**Child Quest International**
1625 The Alameda
Suite 400
San Jose, CA 95126
Tel: 800-248-8020

# INDEX

## Photocredits

Front cover and pages 3, 6 top and bottom, 7, 10, 12 bottom, 19 top and bottom, 20, 22 bottom, 23, 29 top and bottom: Roger Vlitos; pages 4, 9 top and bottom, 12 top, 22 top, 25 top and bottom, 26: Paul Seheult/Eye Ubiquitous; 13, 30: Topham Picture Library; 16: Liz White; 17: Hulton Deutsch.